SO NOW YOU'RE ON YOUR OWN...

A COOKBOOK
FOR COLLEGE STUDENTS AND SINGLES

Easy Recipes
Menus
Helpful Hints
Shopping Hints
Need to Know

Sandra Shaner

SO NOW YOU'RE ON YOUR OWN...

Sandra Shaner

authorHOUSE®

AuthorHouse™
1663 Liberty Drive
Bloomington, IN 47403
www.authorhouse.com
Phone: 1-800-839-8640

Illustrations by Lance Spitler

First published by AuthorHouse   2/7/2011

ISBN: 978-1-4567-3049-9 (sc)
ISBN: 978-1-4567-3050-5 (e)

Library of Congress Control Number: 2011901055

Printed in the United States of America

IN APPRECIATION

My deepest appreciation goes to my grandchildren Brittany, Mason, Emma, Hailey and Noah who inspired me to write this cookbook. They are of college age and encouraged me to help them with easy recipes and cost saving menus.

Special thanks are given to my sons Lance and Jason, for their loving interest and encouragement and to my sister Frances and friend Joan for their contributions to this collection of recipes.

I would also like to thank my husband for tasting the recipes and putting up with all my hours at the computer.

Sandra Shaner

CONTENTS

RECIPES

NEED TO KNOW—NOW

1. You will need three basic pans: a 10 inch cast iron skillet, a saucepan with a lid and a cookie sheet with an edge around it. A one quart casserole dish with a lid would be helpful, but not necessary.

2. You must season your cast iron skillet. You can buy them already seasoned, but the cost is higher. Coat your skillet with cooking oil; use a paper towel to spread it around. Bake it in the oven for 1 hour. IT IS NOW SEASONED. After using it awhile it will turn black and this is what you want. After each use make sure it is completely dry or it will rust. Lightly oil the inside after it is dry. You will use this skillet for frying, baking and roasting.

3. Don't have a rolling pin? Use a can of veggies wrapped in foil or plastic wrap.

4. When you are ready to go shopping for groceries, make up your menu first then your shopping list. See the MENU AND SHOPPING LIST CHAPTER.

5. Boxed pasta meals will give you 3 or 4 days of meals. The directions say to add hamburger or tuna. You can omit the meat and still have a great seasoned pasta meal. You can always add some of your own seasonings or diced onion to make it your own recipe.

6. Try shopping for canned goods, produce and paper products at one of those discount stores—you will save a lot of money.

7. Don't have a lid for your skillet—cover it with foil.

8. If you don't have a strainer, cover pan with the lid, move lid back about ½ an inch and carefully pour out hot water, away from you.

BASICS FOR YOUR KITCHEN

SPICES AND FOOD BASICS

- Salt (I use coarse sea salt) (you can buy a picnic set with salt & pepper)
- Pepper (I like the pepper from a grinder)
- Garlic powder (not garlic salt, otherwise you end up with to much salt in your recipe)
- Onion powder (not onion salt for the same reason)
- Extra virgin olive oil
- Ketchup
- Sweet pickle relish
- Parmesan cheese (the Parmesan & Romano blend is good too)
- Beef cubes
- Season all (several different spices in one container)
- Pancake, biscuit mix
- Dried onion soup (makes great gravy and sauces)

> ### HINT:
>
> Buy a different spice each week, to keep your cost down. Some spices to have are: Chile powder, Italian seasoning, cumin, Cajun seasoning, and small bottle of vinegar. You will figure out other spices as you cook. You can buy salt and pepper in the picnic size to save money.

PANS AND UTENSILS

- Cast iron skillet
- Sauce pan with lid
- Cookie sheet with lip or edge
- Paring knife
- Spatula
- Measuring cup
- Measuring spoons (if you don't have them---guess!)
- Can opener
- Pot holders
- Cutting board
- Aluminum foil (heavy duty)
- Large (1 gallon) zippered plastics bags
- Plastic food storage containers with lids
- 1 quart casserole dish with lid
- Strainer

DOUBLE DUTY FOODS

Canned tomatoes (15 oz)

The tomatoes come plain, seasoned, whole, diced etc.

Use for: Chile, spaghetti, salsa, casserole, roasts.

Dried noodles (small pkg.)

They come in different widths, I use medium. Use what you need and store the rest in a zippered bag.

Use for: stroganoff, casseroles, or just seasoned as a side dish.

Canned Mixed Vegetables (15oz)

Use for: soups, Sheppard pie, hamburger surprise, stew, side dish.

Boxed pancake mix

Use for: pizza dough, dumplings, pancakes, crusts, waffles.

Individual fruit cups

They come four to a package.

Use for: dessert, with gelatin, fruit sauce.

Crackers

Use the buttery ones.

Use for: snacks, crumbled up for bread crumbs.

Orange marmalade

Use for: toast, meat glaze, stuffed in a biscuit.

FOOD TIPS

1. Fry foods on low or medium to minimize clean up.

2. Fry without a lid.

3. Season food as you prepare it.

4. Buy 1 large yellow onion, dice it and freeze what you don't use.

5. Store leftovers in a covered plastic food container in refrigerator.

6. Add leftover meats and vegetables to soup or an omelet.

7. Small amounts of vegetables can be purchased at the salad bar in your grocery store. (mushrooms, shredded cheese, green peppers, olives, dressings, etc)

8. Don't have the time to cook a chicken breast? Buy it in a can.

9. Sausage comes in patties, links and bulk packages and can be used instead of hamburger.

10. Cheese is good in a lot of different recipes. Try different cheeses and utilize the new shredded 3 or 4 cheese blends.

11. **Experiment** with your recipes, if you don't like a certain ingredient-omit it. You can also add to a recipe. Make it yours.

12. Spaghetti leftovers can be stored in water in a covered container in the refrigerator. To warm it up just put in a strainer and run hot water over it.

13. You can buy mashed potatoes ready to heat, they come plain or garlic.

14. When I use the term "butter" in the recipes it also means margarine.

TERMINOLOGY

Crumbled: break up into smaller pieces.

Diced: cut up into small squares.

Dredge: take a food item and coat it with a dry ingredient.

Fry: cook something in a small amount of oil.

Knead: work something with your hands, like dough.

Optional: add or omit something to your recipe.

Minced: dice up something very fine.

Pre heat: turn on the oven or pan and heat it up to a certain temperature.

Simmer: cook something on a low heat.

To taste: adding an ingredient to your liking, like salt.

Toss: to mix several ingredients together lightly.

ABBREVIATIONS

oz	ounce	lg.	large
tsp.	teaspoon	sm.	small
tbsp.	tablespoon	hr.	hour
gal.	gallon	min.	minutes
pkg.	package		

HOW TO DICE AN ONION

1. Cut ends off of large onion.

2. Sit onion on one of the cut ends. Cut onion in half and peel off skin.

3. Lay half onion on cutting board with the small cut end toward you. Now make ¼ inch slices across the onion.

4. Turn the onion so the slices are sideways and do the ¼ inch slices again. You now have diced onion. You can dice the other half and use it or freeze it.

Onions add a lot of flavor to your recipes. I personally use yellow onions. But you can use white or red. The red onions are sweeter. One large onion will last you quite awhile. If you don't have an onion you can always use onion powder or dried onion flakes.

CHICKEN

HINTS

1. Chicken breasts usually come in packages of two or more. Use one and freeze the rest.

2. You could cook both and freeze one.

3. Boneless chicken breasts can be cut into inch strips or one inch cubes (nuggets).

4. When you think your chicken is done cooking, press with a fork. If the juices run clear it is ready to eat. If the juices are pink, cook the chicken a little longer.

5. Always wash your hands thoroughly with soap after handling raw meat. I use a different cutting board for my chicken. Clean cutting board thoroughly.

BAKED BEER CHICKEN PACKET

- 1 chicken breast, boneless
- ¼ tsp. garlic powder
- ¼ tsp. onion powder
- ¼ tsp. salt
- 1/8 tsp. pepper
- ¼ cup beer or chicken broth

YOU WILL NEED

- Oven on 350 degrees
- Skillet
- Aluminum foil
- Measuring spoons and cup

1. Mix all spices; don't forget you can add your own. Sprinkle over chicken.

2. Place chicken on square of foil, push foil up to make an open bowl. Add liquid of choice. Bring up all the edges of the foil bowl to close it tightly. Place packet in skillet and place in oven. Bake for 1 hour.

SERVES: 1

SERVING HINTS: You could add canned mixed vegetables to bottom of packet. You could serve it with French Fries or mashed potatoes. (A little messy but good).

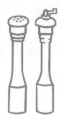

BBQ CHICKEN

- 1 boneless chicken breast cut into 1 inch strips
- ½ cup BBQ sauce (save the rest for other recipes) Put unused sauce in refrigerator.
- ¼ tsp. salt
- ¼ tsp. pepper
- ¼ tsp. garlic powder
- Spray oil or oil for lightly covering foil lined cookie sheet

YOU WILL NEED

- Oven at 450 degrees
- Foil lined cookie sheet
- Fork
- Spoon
- Measuring spoons and cup

1. Oil foil lined cookie sheet. Place chicken strips a couple of inches apart and place in oven. Bake for 30 minutes. Take out of oven.

2. Pour or spoon BBQ sauce over chicken and put back in oven. Bake for another 10 minutes.

SERVES: 1

SERVING HINTS: Serve with French Fries or/and salad. (If using as a finger food, save the homework until you are done).

BUFFALO NUGGETS

- 1 pkg. chicken strips cut into 1 ½ inch pieces (or take 1 chicken breast and cut it up)
- 2 tbsp. hot pepper sauce
- 2 tbsp. water
- ¾ cup pancake mix
- ½ tsp. garlic powder
- 1 tsp. season all
- ½ tsp. salt
- ¼ tsp. pepper

YOU WILL NEED

- Oven at 350 degrees
- 2 bowls
- Foil lined cookie sheet
- Fork, it you don't want to use your fingers.
- Measuring spoons and cup

1. Mix water and hot sauce.

2. Put chicken pieces in bowl with water, hot sauce mixture and let soak for 10 to 15 min.

3. Mix pancake mix and dry spices and put in a bowl.

4. Dredge chicken in pancake mixture.

5. Place coated chicken on oiled foil lined cookie sheet.

6. Bake 30 to 40 minutes until done.

SERVES: 1 OR 2

SERVING HINTS: These would be great with blue cheese or ranch dressing. Serve with French Fries or a salad.

CAJUN CHICKEN AND RICE

⅔ (spicy) ⅔

- 2 chicken breasts
- 1 tsp. garlic powder
- 1 tsp. Cajun seasoning
- 1 cup white rice, instant
- 1 can (14.5 oz.) diced tomatoes with green peppers and onions
- ¾ cup water
- ¼ cup diced onion

YOU WILL NEED

- Oven at 425 degrees
- Foil lined cookie sheet
- Saucepan
- Small bowl
- Measuring spoons and cup
- Can opener

1. Combine spices in small bowl

2. Place chicken on foil lined cookie sheet.

3. Rub spice mixture all over chicken.

4. Bake 40 min. or until juices run clear.

5. Combine rice, tomatoes, water and onion in saucepan, bring to a boil, reduce heat, cover. Simmer 20 minutes or until liquid is absorbed by rice. Stir and serve with chicken.

SERVES: 2

SERVING HINTS: Eat one portion and refrigerate leftovers. You could cut up the leftover chicken and serve it over a salad. The chicken would also be great on a sandwich.

CHICKEN ALA KING

(creamy)

- 1 chicken breast cooked and diced (you can fry, bake or boil the chicken)
- 1 can (10 ¾ oz.) mushroom soup or cream of chicken soup
- ¼ cup milk
- ¼ tsp. salt
- ¼ tsp. pepper

YOU WILL NEED

- Saucepan
- Spoon
- Measuring spoons and cup

1. Put cooked diced chicken in saucepan; add soup, spices and milk. Heat on low until the mixture is hot.

SERVES: 2

SERVING HINTS: This is great served over toast. You could also serve it over rice, spaghetti, mashed potatoes or noodles. It would go good with a salad.

CHICKEN BAKE

- 1 cooked chicken breast or 1 can chicken
- 1 can (10 ¾ oz.) cream of chicken soup
- 1 can (15 oz.) mixed vegetables
- ¼ tsp. salt
- ¼ tsp. pepper
- ¼ tsp. garlic powder
- ¼ cup milk
- ¼ cup shredded cheddar cheese (remember the salad bar at grocery)

YOU WILL NEED

- Oven at 425 degrees
- Iron skillet
- Lid
- Lg. spoon
- Lg. bowl
- Measuring spoons and cup
- Can opener

1. Mix all ingredients, put in your skillet, cover and bake for 20 to 30 minutes until everything is heated through.

SERVES: 1 OR 2

SERVING HINTS: Serve with salad. This is also a good time to experiment with different cheeses.

CHICKEN NUGGETS

- 1 chicken breast, cut into 1 inch pieces
- 1/8 cup olive oil
- ½ cup bread crumbs or cracker crumbs
- ¼ tsp. salt
- ¼ tsp. pepper
- ¼ tsp. garlic powder
- 2 tbsp. Parmesan cheese

YOU WILL NEED

- Oven at 425 degrees
- Sharp knife
- 2 plastic bags or 2 sm. Bowls
- Foil lined cookie sheet
- Measuring spoons and cup

1. Coat chicken pieces with oil (you can put the oil in a bag or bowl).

2. Mix crumbs, spices and cheese in bag or bowl, add chicken and coat well.

3. Arrange chicken pieces on foil lined cookie sheet and bake for 25. to 35 min. or until chicken is done.

SERVES: 1

SERVING HINTS: You could serve this with French fries, salad or veggie. You could also serve a dipping sauce with it (BBQ, cocktail sauce, blue cheese dressing or Ranch dressing).

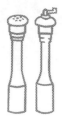

CHICKEN PITA PIZZA

- 1. Chicken breast, cooked and sliced or 1 can pre-cooked chicken
- 2. pita flat breads
- ¼ cup pizza sauce
- ¼ cup shredded mozzarella cheese
- ¼ cup diced onion

1. Place both pitas flat on foil lined cookie sheet, cover with chicken, sauce, cheese and onion.

2. Bake for 5 to 10 min. or until cheese is melted.

SERVES: 1 OR 2

SERVING HINTS: You can eat one and freeze one. This would be good with chips or a salad. It is also easy to eat while you are cramming for that big test.

CHICKEN POT PIE

- 1 chicken breast cooked and diced (boiled, fried, or baked) or 1 can pre-cooked chicken
- 1 can (15 oz.) mixed vegetables
- 1 can (10 ¾ oz) cream of chicken soup
- 1 small potato, diced
- ¼ cup diced onion
- ¼ tsp. salt
- ¼ tsp. pepper
- 1 frozen pie crust, thawed

YOU WILL NEED

- Oven to 350 degrees
- Casserole dish
- Lg. spoon
- Measuring spoons and cup
- Can opener

1. Mix first 7 ingredients in casserole dish.

2. Put thawed pie crust over mixture, fold excess dough back inside the dish or cut off excess.

3. Bake for 30 to 40 min. or until crust is golden brown.

SERVES: 1 OR 2

SERVING HINTS: This is a meal by itself. You could serve it with a salad and bread or crackers.

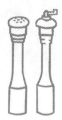

CHICKEN SALAD

- 1 cooked chicken breast, diced
- 1 tbsp. mayonnaise
- ¼ cup onion diced
- 2 tbsp. pickle relish or 1 pickle diced
- 2 tbsp. celery
- ¼ tsp. salt
- ¼ tsp. pepper

YOU WILL NEED

- Lg. bowl
- Spoon
- Knife
- Measuring spoons and cup

1. Mix all ingredients.

SERVES: 1 OR 2

SERVING HINTS: You can pick up pickles and celery at the salad bar in your local grocery. You can eat this as a sandwich or by itself. Serve with potato chips, salad or crackers. If it isn't moist enough just add some more mayonnaise.

CRUNCHY OVEN CHICKEN

- ½ cup corn flakes, crushed
- ½ cup bread crumbs or cracker crumbs
- 1 tsp. sugar
- ¼ tsp. salt
- ¼ tsp. pepper
- 2 tbsp. oil
- 1 pkg. chicken tenders or 1 chicken breast cut into strips
- ¼ cup pancake mix
- 1 egg beaten

YOU WILL NEED

- Oven at 350 degrees
- Plate
- Foil lined cookie sheet
- Fork
- Measuring spoons and cup

1. Pour corn flake crumbs, bread crumbs, sugar, salt, pepper in a plate and mix with fork.

2. Drizzle oil over crumb mixture, tossing to get oil evenly over all of the mixture.

3. Coat chicken in pancake mix, then in egg and then in the crumb mixture. Arrange coated chicken on foil lined cookie sheet. Place in oven and bake for 30 to 40 minutes or until chicken is no longer pink in the center.

SERVES: 1 OR 2

SERVING HINTS: Serve with mashed potatoes (buy them already mixed and ready to heat). A salad or vegetable would be good with the chicken. Remember you can add other spices (Cajun, garlic, season-all). Another great finger food, so you can eat and study at the same time.

FRIED CHICKEN

- 1 chicken breast
- ¼ cup pancake mix, bread crumbs or cracker crumbs
- ¼ tsp. salt
- ¼ tsp. pepper
- ¼ tsp. garlic powder
- ¼ tsp. season-all or Cajun seasoning
- ¾ cup vegetable oil

YOU WILL NEED

- Iron cast skillet
- Fork
- Bowl for mixing pancake mix and spices
- Measuring spoons and cup

1. Mix pancake mix and spices in bowl.

2. Rub chicken with a little of the oil, pour rest into skillet and start heating .

3. Dredge chicken with dry mixture.

4. Add chicken to hot oil, slowly put end of chicken in oil and lay it in away from you. You are less likely to get splashed with hot oil that way.

5. Cook until golden brown and turn over, brown other side. Remove and put on a paper towel to drain. Make sure it is done; press with fork for clear juices.

SERVES: 1

SERVING HINTS: Serve with mashed potatoes, salad and/or a vegetable. French fries would be good with the chicken. Save any leftover mashed potatoes for potato patties or potato candy.

ITALIAN CHICKEN SANDWICH

- 1 chicken breast, boneless
- ¼ cup pancake mix
- ¼ cup grated parmesan cheese
- ½ tsp. Italian seasoning
- ¼ cup water
- 1 slice mozzarella cheese (remember the salad bar)
- 2 tbsp. oil
- ¼ cup spaghetti sauce
- Bread or bun

YOU WILL NEED

- 2 bowls
- Skillet
- Fork
- Knife
- Measuring spoons and cup

1. Butterfly (cut <u>almost</u> in half sideways, so it looks like a book) chicken, open it up and dip into water (you could use oil).

2. Mix pancake mix, parmesan cheese and spices.

3. Add oil to skillet over medium heat. When hot, add coated chicken and fry until a golden brown turn the chicken over and brown other side. It is done when the juices run clear.

4. Put mozzarella slice over chicken and top with spaghetti sauce. Heat long enough to warm sauce. Place on bread or bun and enjoy.

SERVES: 1

SERVING HINTS: A salad or chips would be good with this sandwich. (Not to be eaten near homework as the sauce laden paper is no excuse for not turning it in).

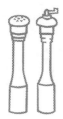

ORANGE CHICKEN

- 2 chicken breasts or 1 pkg. chicken tenders
- 1/3 cup pancake mix
- ½ tsp. salt
- ¼ tsp. pepper
- ½ cup oil
- 1/3 cup diced onion
- 1/3 cup of orange juice concentrate (make orange juice with the rest)
- ¼ cup water

YOU WILL NEED

- Oven at 350 degrees
- Skillet with lid
- Bowl
- Lg. spoon
- Plate
- Measuring spoons and cup

1. Combine pancake mix, spices and dredge chicken on all sides.

2. Brown coated chicken in oil on both sides, when golden brown, remove to a plate and add onions to skillet and sauté until soft. Add orange juice concentrate and water. Add chicken and spoon with the mixture. Cover with lid or foil.

3. Bake for 45 min. to an hour.

SERVES: 3 TO 4

SERVING HINTS: This is fantastic with mashed potatoes, as you can use the orange juice mixture as gravy. The leftover chicken can be used as sandwiches or cut up and made into a tasty chicken salad.

ORANGE CHICKEN PACKET

- 1 chicken breast
- ½ can (15 oz.) mixed vegetables (refrigerate other half)
- 2 tbsp. orange marmalade
- ¼ tsp. salt
- 1/8 tsp. pepper

1. Shape foil into bowl shape, add vegetables, and sprinkle with half the spices.

2. Put chicken on top of the vegetables, sprinkle with rest of spices, then spread marmalade over the top of the chicken.

3. Close up packet, place on foil lined cookie sheet and bake for 1 hour.

SERVES: 1

SERVING HINTS: This is pretty much a meal in one. But you could add a salad or potatoes. If you have a study buddy you just double the recipe

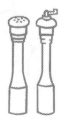

ORIENTAL CHICKEN

- 2 chicken breasts
- Vegetable oil to fill skillet up to ½ inch
- ½ cup diced onion
- 1 chicken cube dissolved in 1 cup boiling water
- 2 tbsp. soy sauce
- 1 tbsp. lemon juice
- 1 tbsp. brown sugar
- 1 tbsp. cornstarch

YOU WILL NEED

- Skillet
- Lid (If you don't have a lid, use foil).
- Plate
- Measuring spoons and cup

1. Brown chicken in oil until golden brown, remove from oil and set aside.

2. Sauté onions in same oil and then add rest of ingredients, cook over medium heat and stir constantly until thick.

3. Put chicken back in mixture, cover and simmer for 10 to 15 minutes.

SERVES: 1 OR 2

REFRIGERATE WHAT YOU DON'T USE. YOU CAN REHEAT OR CUT UP THE CHICKEN FOR ANOTHER DISH.

SERVING HINTS: This would be good with rice. Cut up your chicken and practice using chop sticks.

STUFFED CHICKEN BREAST

- 1 chicken breast
- ¼ tsp. salt
- ¼ tsp. pepper
- ¼ tsp. garlic powder
- 1 sm. Can fruit cocktail or ¼ cup leftover rice, leftover vegetables, ½ apple sliced
- ¼ cup water

YOU WILL NEED

- Oven at 350 degrees
- Skillet
- Aluminum foil
- Spoon
- Foil lined cookie sheet
- Knife
- Measuring spoons and cup

1. Slice the chicken lengthwise to make a hole for the stuffing. Add the stuffing of your choice. You could mix 2 different stuffing, like apple and vegetables or rice and fruit. Sprinkle with spices.

2. Form aluminum foil into a bowl shape, add stuffed chicken and ¼ cup water. Place on foil lined cookie sheet.

3. Bake for 45 – 55 minutes or until chicken is no longer pink in center.

SERVES: 1

SERVING HINTS: This is a recipe you could go wild with. Try using marmalade or peanut butter for stuffing.

CHUCK ROAST

HINTS

1. There are several types of beef roasts. I think that the chuck roast is the more flavorful and tender.

2. When you get your roast home you can cut it into three or four pieces use one and freeze the rest. Wrap them well. You can also cook the whole roast and then freeze what you don't use.

3. The secret to a tender and tasty roast is to sear it in the oven almost to the point where it looks almost burnt. Then cook it, covered, low and slow for six or seven hours. Check it once in awhile to make sure it has plenty of liquid.

BBQ CHUCK SANDWICHES

- 1 cup leftover roast, pulled or cut into bite sizes
- ¼ cup BBQ sauce
- ¼ tsp. salt
- ¼ tsp. pepper
- Bread or a bun

YOU WILL NEED

- Skillet
- Lg. spoon
- Measuring spoons and cup

1. Add first 4 ingredients to skillet, simmer, on low, until everything is hot.

SERVES: 1

SERVING HINTS: Serve with chips and Cole slaw (the salad bar is a great place to get just 1 helping of slaw). It is also good as an open faced sandwich.

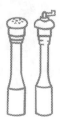

BEEF AND NOODLES

- 1/3 of that roast you bought, you can cook it whole and then cut it into bite sizes
- ¼ cup oil
- 2 ½ cups water
- ½ tsp. salt
- ¼ tsp. pepper
- ½ tsp. garlic powder
- ½ cup onion, diced
- 2 beef cubes
- 2 cups noodles, uncooked

YOU WILL NEED

- Skillet
- Lg. spoon
- Knife
- Measuring spoons and cup

1. Heat oil in skillet, add roast and sear on both sides

2. Add rest of ingredients except noodles, cover, and simmer on low for at least 3 hours (this is the time to work on your homework, read a book or clean the apartment).

3. Add the noodles and continue to cook until noodles are tender, about 20 to 30 minutes.

SERVES: 2 OR 3

SERVING HINTS: This can also be made in a Dutch oven if you have one. You can also add other spices (thyme, oregano, season-all etc.). The leftovers are just as good as the first day you made the dish.

BEEF HASH

- 1 cup leftover roast, cut or torn into bite size pieces
- 1 cup leftover vegetables from roast or 1 can (15 oz.) mixed vegetables
- ¼ cup diced onions
- 1 or 2 beef cubes
- ½ cup water

YOU WILL NEED

- Skillet
- Spoon
- Measuring cup or just eyeball it
- Measuring spoons

1. Add all ingredients to skillet; simmer on low until all ingredients are hot.

SERVES: 1 OR 2

SERVING HINTS: This is good as is. You could serve it with salad and/or crusty bread. If there are any leftovers, heat it up and pour over noodles or rice. Helps stretch that dollar which you could use for books.

BEEF STEW

- ¼ cup oil
- 1/3 roast cut into bite size pieces (you could use leftover roast with the juice)
- ¼ cup onion, diced
- ½ cup celery, diced (don't forget the local grocery salad bar)
- 1 medium potato, diced
- 1 cup carrots cut into bite size pieces (salad bar again)
- 2 cups water
- 2 beef cubes
- ½ tsp. salt
- ½ tsp. pepper
- ½ tsp. garlic powder

YOU WILL NEED

- Skillet or Dutch oven
- Lid
- Lg. spoon
- Measuring spoons and cup

1. If using raw roast, sear the pieces, in oil, on all sides until really brown, on medium heat. Turn heat to low and add onions. If using leftover roast don't fry, just add all ingredients to skillet and simmer for about 1 hour.

2. Add rest of ingredients, cover and simmer for 2 or 3 hours. Check once in awhile to make sure there is enough liquid, if not add a little at a time.

SERVES: 2 OR 3

SERVING HINTS: This is great with "dippy" bread. It is what I call crusty bread. Just dip it into the gravy and enjoy. Not a good thing to do at a restaurant—but in your own home, you rule.

BEEF STIR FRY

- 1 cup leftover roast with juices
- ¼ cup stir-fry sauce
- ½ bag stir fry vegetables (freeze the other half, use for vegetable soup later)
- 1 cup cooked ramen noodles
- ¼ tsp. salt
- ¼ tsp. pepper

1. Heat skillet and add beef, juices, stir fry sauce and vegetables. Stir and cook for 6 to 8 minutes until vegetables are no longer frozen. Prepare noodles while the mixture is heating.

2. Serve meat mixture over noodles.

SERVES: 1 OR 2

SERVING HINTS: If you have Soy sauce, sprinkle some over stir fry. You could serve this with a salad. Don't like noodles? Use some of that rice in your pantry. Remember, it is your kitchen and you rule!

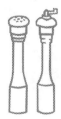

CHUCK ROAST CHILE

- 1 cup leftover roast cut
  into bites size pieces
- 1 can chili starter (it has
  beans, sauce and spices)
- 1 can (15oz.) diced tomatoes
  (plain or spiced)
- Shredded cheese is optional

YOU WILL NEED

- Cast iron skillet
- Lg. spoon
- Bowl
- Measuring cup
- Can opener

1. Put all ingredients into skillet,
   except cheese. Heat ingredients on low or medium until
   everything is hot then put into a bowl and sprinkle with
   cheese.

SERVES: 1 OR 2

SERVING HINTS: Serve with some crackers
and you have a meal that is satisfying and filling.
I use shredded sharp cheddar cheese, but you
could use mild cheddar, mozzarella or even
Swiss.

CHUCK ROAST

This recipe takes several hours to cook so you can do homework, clean the apartment or just be a couch potato. It is very low maintenance.

YOU WILL NEED

- Oven at 350 degrees
- Cast iron skillet
- Lid or foil
- Lg. spoon
- Knife

- 1 small chuck roast (you can fix all of it or divide into thirds and freeze the rest) If you fix it all you can use the rest for sandwiches, hash etc.)
- ¼ cup oil
- 1 med. onion, diced or sliced
- ½ tsp. garlic powder
- ½ tsp. salt
- ¼ tsp. pepper
- ½ tsp. season-all
- 1 lg. potato, cut into halves
- ½ bag of baby carrots
- 2 cups water

1. Put oil in skillet and add the roast. Put in oven and brown on both sides. Let it get <u>really dark brown</u> on both sides, this is what gives you the flavor. Add water, spices and onion. Cover and bake for 4 hours. Check after 2 hours to make sure there is enough water to cover at least ½ inch of the bottom of the skillet.

2. Add the carrots, check the juices and bake for another hour.

3. Add the potatoes, check the juices again and bake for another hour or until the carrots are tender.

SERVES: 1 OR MORE

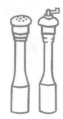

SERVING HINTS: You can add salt and pepper to the potato and carrots. You could also add a beef cube at any time for more intense flavor.

CHUCK ROAST SANDWICH

This is an open faced sandwich.

- ¾ cup leftover roast with about ¼ cup of the juices
- 1 beef cube
- 1 cup water
- ¼ cup onion, diced
- ¼ cup shredded cheddar cheese (or cheese of your choice)
- ¼ tsp. salt
- ¼ tsp. pepper
- 1 slice of bread

YOU WILL NEED

- Cast iron skillet
- Lg. spoon
- Knife

1. Put water and beef cube in skillet on low, when the cube has dissolved add beef, onion and spices. Simmer until beef is hot.

2. Layer beef and cheese on bread, top with the juice from the skillet.

SERVES: 1

SERVING HINTS: Try serving this with potato chips and a pickle. Cole slaw or cottage cheese would be good with it too. If you have leftover potatoes or carrots from the roast, heat them up in the skillet with the beef and pout it all over the bread. If there are no beef juices left, just use the beef cube and water.

DESSERTS

BAKED APPLES

- 2 Granny Smith apples (the green ones)
- ¼ cup brown sugar
- ¼ tsp. cinnamon
- 1 cup water

YOU WILL NEED

- Bowl
- Spoon or whisk
- Sauce pan or microwavable cup

1. Wash apples and remove the cores within ½ inch of the bottom.

2. Place apples, core side up, in skillet. If they won't sit up right, trim a little off the bottom. Fill centers with brown sugar and cinnamon.

3. Add water to skillet and bake for 30 to 45 minutes until apples are tender.

SERVES: 2

SERVING HINTS: Have one now and refrigerate one for later.

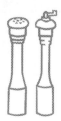

BANANA PUDDING

- 1 small (4 oz.) pkg. instant vanilla pudding
- 1 small box of vanilla wafers
- 2 cups milk
- 2 bananas

YOU WILL NEED

- 2 bowls (one for mixing and one for serving)
- Lg. spoon or whisk
- Knife

1. Mix vanilla pudding according to pkg. directions.

2. Cut banana into slices, sideways.

3. Place some wafers on bottom and sides of the other bowl, add some banana slices and spoon in some pudding, repeat until all the pudding is used. Top with wafers. Make sure the bananas are covered with pudding or they will turn brown. Refrigerate.

SERVES: 4

SERVING HINTS: You can eat it right away and refrigerate the rest, just make sure you cover it with a lid or plastic wrap. You can snack on the leftover wafers or make some strawberry spread and have some tasty dessert snacks later on. If you want to make the pudding a little richer you could add some vanilla extract if you have it.

CAKE MIX COOKIES

- 1 box cake mix (your favorite: lemon, strawberry, chocolate)
- 2 eggs
- 1/2 cup vegetable oil

YOU WILL NEED

- Oven to 350 degrees
- Mixing bowl
- Lg. spoon
- Foil lined cookie sheet
- Spatula or fork

1. Mix all ingredients, <u>mix well.</u>

2. Place by spoonfuls on foil lined cookie sheet about 1 ½ inches apart.

3. Bake for 7-9 minutes, until center springs back when touched lightly (and quickly).

4. Cool and store in an airtight plastic container.

SERVES: 4 OR 5
(depends on how much they like them).

SERVING HINTS: You could add nuts or raisins to the batter, if you like, or a splash of vanilla extract. You could also buy a tub of icing in whatever flavor you like and have iced cookies (very rich). If you have some jam or jelly you could put a tsp. on top of the cookies. You could even put some peanut butter on them.

CINNAMON WEDGES

- 2 tbsp. sugar
- 1 tsp. cinnamon
- 4 8 inch tortillas
- 3 tbsp. butter or margarine

YOU WILL NEED

- Oven on 400 degrees
- Foil lined cookie sheet
- Small bowl
- Knife
- Fork

1. Put butter on foil lined cookie sheet and put in oven.

2. While the butter is melting, mix sugar and cinnamon in bowl.

3. Cut tortillas into 8 wedges.

4. Carefully pull cookie sheet out of oven. Put wedges in butter and turn over to coat on both sides, sprinkle with sugar mixture. Return to oven and bake for 4 to 6 minutes.

SERVES: 1 OR 2

SERVING HINTS: Store any leftover wedges in an air tight container. Great for late night snacking or while you are doing homework.

FRUIT CRISP

Thanks to my friend Joan

- 1 can pie fruit (peach, cherry or apple)
- 1 sm. Box cake mix (yellow or white)
- ½ tsp. cinnamon (optional)
- 4 tbsp. melted butter

YOU WILL NEED

- Oven at 350 degrees
- Small bowl
- Spoon
- Can opener
- 8 inch cake pan

1. Put fruit in the bottom of the cake pan.

2. Mix melted butter and cake mix and crumble over the fruit.

3. Bake for 30 to 45 minutes until top is golden brown.

SERVES: 4 -6

SERVING HINTS: Try using different measures of butter, the less you use the more it will be like crusty crumbles, the more butter you use the more it will be like a cake topping. This would not only be good alone but try it with some ice cream or whipped cream.

FRUIT PIZZA

Save this one for when you are having friends over. Refreshing and easy.

- 1 pkg. (17oz.) sugar cookie dough (cut in half, wrap and refrigerate the other half)
- 1 pkg. (8 oz.) cream cheese, room temperature (cut in half, wrap and refrigerate the other half)
- 1 cup fresh fruit, cut into thin bite sizes (remember the salad bar) your favorites
- ½ cup jam (orange, strawberry)

YOU WILL NEED

- Oven at 350 degrees
- Cookie sheet
- Knife
- Sauce pan
- Spoon

1. Roll out cookie dough (use a foil covered can of vegetables if you don't have a rolling pin). Put dough on the cookie sheet and bake for 8 to 15 minutes, or until dough is done.

2. Let cool then spread with the cream cheese and arrange fruit on top of the cream cheese.

3. Warm marmalade or jam in the sauce pan and drizzle over the fruit.

SERVES: 2 OR MORE

SERVING HINTS: Later you could make cookies out of the leftover cookie dough. The leftover cream cheese can be spread on crackers or mixed with a little jam to make a spread of its own. What ever type of fruit you like would be good on your pizza. Experiment!

GELATIN AND FRUIT

- 1 pkg. flavored gelatin
- 2 cups water
- 1 container (4 oz.) fruit,
  they come in sets of four

1. Fix gelatin like it says on the pkg., add fruit and put in
   refrigerator until set.

SERVES: 2 OR MORE

SERVING HINTS: You could also add nuts, raisins, or marshmallows. Crumble some leftover cookies on top. This makes a light and refreshing dessert or late night snack.

MACAROONS

- 8 oz. Shredded coconut
- 1 sm. Can sweetened condensed milk
- 1 tsp. Vanilla

YOU WILL NEED

- Oven at 350 degrees
- Foil lined cookie sheet
- Lg. bowl
- Lg. spoon

1. Mix all ingredients and drop by tbsp. on the foil lined cookie sheet, about an inch apart.

2. Bake for about 8 minutes, just till the tops start to get brown. Cool

SERVES: 4 OR MORE

SERVING HINTS: If you have any chocolate syrup, drizzle the macaroons with some of it or drop a little jam on each macaroon.

ORANGE BALL COOKIES

No cooking on this recipe.

- 2 cups vanilla wafer, crumbled fine
- ½ pkg. (8oz.) powdered sugar
- ¾ cup nuts or your choice, chopped
- ½ can (6 oz.) frozen orange juice concentrate, thawed, undiluted
- ¼ cup butter or margarine
- ½ pkg. (7 oz.) coconut

YOU WILL NEED

- Lg. bowl
- Lg. spoon
- Foil lined cookie sheet

1. Mix first 5 ingredients in your bowl, mix well.

2. Shape into bite size balls and roll in coconut, place on cookie sheet and refrigerate. If to moist, just add more crumbled vanilla wafers.

SERVES: 2 OR MORE
(makes about 2 dozen cookies)

SERVING HINTS: If you don't like nuts omit them, you could add raisins instead. Save the balance of the vanilla wafers for banana pudding or eat them with jam or alone.

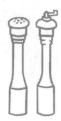

PEANUT BUTTER COOKIES

No bake on this one.

- ½ cup sugar
- ½ cup light corn syrup
- ½ tsp. vanilla extract
- 1 cup peanut butter
- 2 ¼ cups crisp rice cereal

YOU WILL NEED

- Saucepan
- Lg. spoon
- Foil lined cookie sheet

1. Mix the sugar and corn syrup in saucepan, bring to a boil and cook for 1 minute.

2. Remove from the heat and stir in the vanilla and peanut butter, until blended, stir in the cereal and mix well.

3. Drop by spoonful onto the foil lined cookie sheet, cool before serving or storing.

SERVES: 3 OR MORE

(about 1 ½ dozen cookies)

SERVING HINTS: Serve for your friends while you are watching the game or doing homework with a study group.

WHITE CHOCOLATE COOKIES

(No bake)

- 1 cup white chocolate chips
- ¼ cup chunky or smooth peanut butter
- ¾ cup miniature marshmallows
- ½ cup peanuts (salted or unsalted)
- ½ cup toasted rice cereal

YOU WILL NEED

- Oven on 200 degrees
- Lg. spoon
- Foil lined cookie sheet
- Casserole dish

1. Put chocolate in casserole dish and put in oven until melted, remove from oven and add peanut butter and rest of ingredients.

2. Drop by spoonfuls onto foil lined cookie sheet. Cool and store in airtight containers.

SERVES: 2 OR MORE
(makes about 1 dozen cookies)

SERVING HINTS: Any leftover ingredients can be used in other desserts. Although, the chips are good just as they are, eat them like peanuts or mix them with the leftover peanuts and have a party mix.

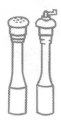

HAM

HINTS
1. Buy one large ham steak and divide it into three or four pieces. Freeze what you don't use. Wrap well.
2. Most ham is precooked but check the label.

GRILLED HAM AND CHEESE

- 1/3 slice of cooked or leftover ham
- 2 slices of cheese of your choice (Swiss, American or cheddar)
- 2 slices of bread
- 2 tsp. butter
- 1 tsp. mustard (optional)

YOU WILL NEED

- Skillet
- Knife
- Spatula

1. Heat skillet on medium, thinly coat 1 side of bread (both slices) with butter

2. Layer ham, cheese and mustard on bread; add other piece of bread (butter sides out)

3. Fry in skillet until bread is brown on both sides

SERVES: 1

SERVING HINTS: This sandwich is really good with tomato soup. You could also serve it with chips. If you like peppers add them to your sandwich just before frying.

Just because the title is Ham and Cheese doesn't mean you can't add what ever you want to make it your creation.

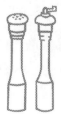

HAM AU GRATIN

1 Pot Meal

- 1 cup ham, cooked and diced
- 1 cup milk
- ½ cup water
- 1 can (11 oz.) corn with peppers, drained
- 1 can (10 ¾ oz.) cheddar cheese soup
- 1 pkg. cheese scalloped potatoes
- ½ tsp. salt
- ¼ tsp. pepper
- ¼ tsp. garlic powder
- ¼ cup diced onions (optional)

YOU WILL NEED

- Oven at 350 degrees
- Skillet with lid or foil
- Lg. spoon
- Can opener

1. Mix all ingredients in skillet, cover and bake until potatoes are soft, about 1 hour.

SERVES: 3 TO 6

SERVING HINTS: A salad would set off this meal perfectly. This is a good recipe to have if you are having friends over.

HAM AND CHEESY SHELLS

1 Pot Meal

- 1/3 cup leftover ham, diced
- 1 pkg. shells and cheese
- 3 cups water

YOU WILL NEED

- Saucepan
- Strainer or lid for saucepan
- Lg. spoon

1. Bring water to boil, add shells and boil until shells are soft, drain and put back into saucepan.

2. Add sauce and ham, stir well.

SERVES: 2 OR MORE

SERVING HINTS: You could add diced onions, shredded cheddar cheese, parmesan cheese and/or top with cracker crumbs. To warm up the next day add a little milk and butter. Store tightly covered.

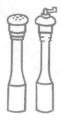

HAM LOAF AND SAUCE

Something different

- 1 ham steak, boned and minced as small as you can get it
- ½ tsp. salt
- ¼ tsp. pepper
- ¼ cup onions, minced
- ½ cup cracker crumbs
- 1 egg
- ½ cup milk

SAUCE

- ½ cup brown sugar
- 1/8 cup water
- 1 tsp. dry mustard (optional)

YOU WILL NEED

- Oven to 350 degrees
- Skillet
- 2 Bowls
- Lg. spoon
- Spatula

1. Mix all the ingredients for ham loaf. Form into an oval (like a flat ended football) and put into skillet. Bake for 1 hour. If it is to wet to form, add more cracker crumbs, if it is to dry add a little more milk.

2. Mix brown sugar and water and pour over loaf after 45 minutes.

SERVES: 3 OR 4

SERVING HINTS: You could have the butcher at the grocery grind the ham for you. Instead of brown sugar and water try a little maple syrup over the ham loaf. This would be good with some canned sweet potatoes, add the brown sugar to them.

HAM PASTA SALAD

This is a cold dish great for picnics.

- 1 cup cooked pasta (shells, elbows etc.), cooled
- ¼ cup onion, diced
- 1/8 cup pickle relish (or diced pickles from the salad bar)
- 1 hard-cooked egg, diced
- ½ cup ham, cooked, diced

YOU WILL NEED

- Lg. spoon
- Lg. bowl

DRESSING

- ¼ cup mayonnaise
- 1 tsp. yellow mustard (save those packets from the fast food places)
- ¼ tsp. salt
- ¼ tsp. pepper

1. Mix all ingredients, put in refrigerator and let it chill.

SERVES: 2 OR 3

SERVING HINTS: This pasta dish can be fixed as a meal or as a side dish. You can always add more ham if you like it meaty. Serve it with crackers or chips. You could also pick up a few fresh vegetables to serve with it (celery, carrots etc.) Remember the salad bar!

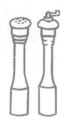

HAM SALAD

For sandwiches

- 1/3 ham steak, cooked and diced small
- 1 tbsp. pickle relish
- 1 tbsp. mayonnaise
- ¼ tsp. salt
- ¼ tsp. pepper

YOU WILL NEED

- Bowl for mixing
- Lg. spoon

1. Mix all ingredients.

SERVES: 1 OR 2

SERVING HINTS: If you have any ham salad left over, try it as a snack on crackers.

HAM SKILLET

1 Pot Meal

- ½ cup ham, cooked, diced (could use leftovers)
- 1 cup uncooked noodles (pasta shells, elbow macaroni, broken up spaghetti)
- ½ tsp. onion powder
- ¼ tsp. salt
- ¼ tsp. pepper
- ½ tsp. Worcestershire sauce
- 1 can (15oz.) creamed corn
- ½ cup American cheese cubed

YOU WILL NEED

- Iron cast skillet
- Lg. spoon
- Can opener

1. Combine all ingredients except cheese, mix well. Bring to a boil, cover and simmer 12 to 15 min. or until noodles or pasta is tender. Stir occasionally.

2. Stir in cheese and simmer until it melts.

SERVES: 1 OR 2

SERVING HINTS: All you need with this would be a salad. If you have some leftover vegetables or potatoes add them to jazz up the dish.

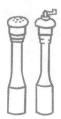

MAPLE HAM AND SWEET POTATOES

Quick meal

- 1/3 ham steak
- ¼ cup maple syrup
- 1 can (15 oz.) sweet potatoes, partially drained
- 1/8 cup cooking oil

YOU WILL NEED

- Skillet
- Lg. spoon
- Fork for turning ham
- Can opener

1. Heat skillet on medium, add oil and ham. Cook on medium until ham is done (see directions on pkg.).

2. Pour maple syrup on ham and turn it over to coat both sides, add sweet potatoes and simmer until potatoes are hot.

SERVES: 1 OR 2

SERVING HINTS: Heat up a green veggie (peas, green beans) to round out your meal. A salad would be good too. Don't have any syrup; add ¼ cup brown sugar and ¼ cup sweet potato juice.

HAM MONTE CRISTO

Something different

- 1 egg
- ¼ cup water
- 1/3 cup flour
- ¾ tsp. baking powder
- 2 slices bread
- 1 slice Swiss cheese (the deli section at the grocery store)
- 1 slice turkey (deli)
- 1 slice ham, sliced thin (deli)
- ¼ tsp. pepper
- ¼ cup jam for dunking
- oil to cover bottom of skillet at least ½ inch

1. Mix flour, baking powder, egg and water to make batter.

2. Assemble sandwich and cut in half, dip into the batter and coat on all sides.

3. Carefully put batter covered sandwich halves into the hot oil and brown on both sides.

SERVES: 1

SERVING HINTS: These sandwiches are usually served with jam on the side or dip the sandwich in the jam. If you don't have flour and baking soda, use your pancake mix instead. Salty chips will counterbalance the sweetness of the sandwich

PEANUT BUTTER GLAZED HAM

- ½ ham steak
- 1 chicken cube, dissolved in ¾ cup boiling water
- ¼ cup peanut butter, smooth or crunchy
- 1/8 cup brown sugar
- ¼ tsp. garlic powder
- 1 tsp. soy sauce (optional)

YOU WILL NEED

- Oven at 325 degrees
- Skillet
- Bowl
- Spoon

1. Place ham steak into skillet.

2. Mix all other ingredients in bowl then pour over ham, cover skillet and place in oven.

3. Bake for 20 to 30 minutes.

SERVES: 2
(1/2 now and the other half as a sandwich)

SERVING HINTS: Slaw and/or sweet potatoes would go well with this.

HAMBURGER

HINTS

1. Take one pound of hamburger (I use ground chuck, it is tastier) and work it lightly with your hands. I do that to get rid of the long strands that were caused the meat grinder. (I won't tell you what my grandchildren say those strands look like).

2. Divide into two, three or four portions. Freeze what you don't use. Wrap well. You can also fry up the whole pound, freeze the rest and use for spaghetti, chili, soup etc.

3. One pound of hamburger can be one patty and one small meatloaf or two patties and beef stroganoff.

BBQ MEATLOAF

- ½ pound hamburger
- ¼ cup bread crumbs, cracker crumbs or uncooked rice
- 1 tsp. onion powder or ¼ cup diced onions
- 1 egg, beaten
- ½ tsp. salt
- ¼ tsp. pepper
- ½ cup BBQ sauce, divided in half

YOU WILL NEED

- Oven on 350 degrees
- Lg. mixing bowl
- Lg. spoon
- Skillet
- Foil to line skillet

1. Mix all ingredients except ½ of BBQ sauce. Form into a rounded football and place in foil lined skillet. Pour remaining BBQ sauce over meatloaf.

2. Bake for 45 to 55 minutes or until meatloaf is no longer pink in center.

SERVES: 1 OR 2

SERVING HINTS: Meatloaf is good with baked potatoes and baked beans. You could also have potato salad and beans. Your kitchen-your choice.

BEEF CHEESY NACHOS

- ½ pound hamburger
- ½ cup salsa (bottled or salad bar)
- 1/3 bag tortilla chips
- 1 cup shredded Mexican style cheese
- Toppings: ¼ cup diced onions, ¼ cup diced tomatoes, diced jalapeños, diced peppers, chopped olives, sour cream (your favorites and remember the salad bar)

1. Brown meat in skillet, stir in salsa and simmer until heated through.

2. Put chips into foil bowl on cookie sheet, top with meat and cheese.

3. Bake until cheese is melted. Remove from oven and top with your favorite toppings.

SERVES: 2

SERVING HINTS: If you have a microwave oven you can nuke the chips and cheese. Every microwave is different so start off on high at one minute and go from there. You just want the cheese to melt.

BEEF TOSTADAS

- ½ pound hamburger
- ¼ cup onion
- ½ tsp. garlic powder
- ½ cup tomatoes, diced
  (remember the salad bar at
  the grocery)
- 2 tostado shells
- ½ cup sour cream
- ¼ tsp. salt
- ¼ tsp. pepper
- ¾ cup shredded cheese (your
  choice)

YOU WILL NEED

- Skillet
- Lg. spoon
- Measuring cups or just
  guess (saves on dishes later)

1. Fry hamburger in skillet, add seasonings. You can add the
   onion now or sprinkle them on top of the tostada raw. (I do
   both, but I love onions).

2. Spoon hamburger on tostada shell then layer everything on top
   ending with the sour cream.

SERVES: 1 OR 2

SERVING HINTS: These are filling but you
could still serve them with a nice crisp salad.

CAJUN BURGER

❧ (spicy) ❧

- ½ pound hamburger
- ¼ cup onion, diced
- ¼ cup bell pepper, diced (any color and remember the salad bar)
- 1 tsp. Worcestershire sauce
- 1 tsp. BBQ sauce
- 2 drops hot sauce (optional)
- 1 tsp. Cajun seasoning
- ½ tsp. garlic powder
- Bun or 2 slices bread

YOU WILL NEED

- Skillet
- Spatula
- Bowl
- Spoon

1. Mix all seasonings, sauces and hamburger. Form into two patties.

2. Fry until done on both sides

SERVES: 2

SERVING HINTS: Wrap the extra burger and refrigerate. It could be warmed up for a sandwich in a couple of days or crumbled and used for soup or any other dish that calls for crumbled hamburger. This would be good with chips or French fries.

CHILI

- 1 pound hamburger
- 1 can (15.5 oz.) chili starter (beans and seasonings)
- 1 can (14.5 tomatoes) they can be diced, flavored, stewed your preference
- ½ tsp. salt
- ½ tsp. pepper
- Optional: ½ cup diced onion, 1 tsp. chili powder, 1 tsp. cumin, 1 can kidney beans

YOU WILL NEED

- Skillet
- Lg. spoon
- Knife
- Can opener
- Measuring spoons or your best guess

1. Fry hamburger on medium, while it is frying add the onions and seasonings.

2. When done add the chili starter, tomatoes and kidney beans. Cook until everything is warmed.

SERVES: 4 OR 5

SERVING HINTS: Serve with crackers. You can also sprinkle a little shredded cheese on top. Chili is always better the next day; the flavors have a chance to blend together. You can also use your chili to top hot dogs (chili dog). Why not top a hamburger with the chili?

GOULASH

- 2 cups leftover chili
- ½ cup pasta, cooked (shells, elbow, broken up spaghetti)
- ½ tsp. paprika (optional)

1. Put all ingredients into your skillet and heat through.

SERVES: 1 OR 2

SERVNG HINTS: This would go great with crackers or a chunk of crusty bread. Cole slaw or salad would be good on the side. Heat up leftovers for lunch the next day.

HAMBURGER CASSEROLE

- ½ pound hamburger
- 1 can (15oz.) mixed vegetables, drained
- ¼ cup onion, diced
- ¼ tsp. salt
- 1.4 tsp. pepper
- ¼ tsp. garlic powder
- 1 can (10 ¾ oz) mushroom soup

YOU WILL NEED

- Skillet
- Lg. spoon
- Can opener

1. Fry hamburger, on medium, until done. Add rest of ingredients, stir well and simmer on low until veggies and soup is hot.

SERVES: 2 TO 4

SERVING HINTS: You could add some shredded cheese just before it gets done or sprinkle the cheese over the top to serve. Depending on whether it is summer or winter you could serve this with potato salad for summer or French Fries for winter.

HAMBURGER CHEESY PIE

- ½ pound hamburger
- ¼ cup onion, diced
- ¼ tsp. garlic powder
- 1 can (15 oz.) corn drained
- 1 can (11 oz.) diced tomatoes with herbs
- 1 frozen pie crust, unthawed
- ¾ cup shredded cheddar cheese

YOU WILL NEED

- Oven at 350 degrees
- Skillet
- Lg. spoon
- Can opener
- Casserole dish

1. Fry hamburger and onion until the meat is done. Add corn and tomatoes. Stir well.

2. Place thawed pie crust into your casserole dish, spoon hamburger mixture into pie shell.

3. Bake for 30-40 minutes or until crust is golden brown. Sprinkle cheese over top and bake an additional 10 minutes.

SERVES: 4-6

SERVING HINTS: This is pretty much a meal in one, the only thing you need to add would be a salad. You could also add some Parmesan cheese on top to layer the flavor factor.

HAMBURGER GRAVY

Topper for toast

- ½ pound hamburger
- 1 can (10 ¾ oz.) mushroom soup
- 1 tsp. Worcestershire sauce
- ½ cup onion, diced
- 1 cup noodles or pasta, cooked (optional, you could use toast)

YOU WILL NEED

- Skillet
- Lg. spoon
- Can opener

1. Fry hamburger and onion, on medium, until meat is done.

2. Add soup and sauce and simmer until everything is hot.

SERVES: 2-4

SERVING HINTS: Serve over noodles, mashed potatoes or toast.

HAMBURGER PATTY

- ¼ pound hamburger
- ¼ tsp. salt
- ¼ tsp. pepper
- ¼ tsp. of any of the following: garlic powder, Cajun seasoning, onion powder, parmesan cheese, shredded cheddar cheese, BBQ sauce, catsup

YOU WILL NEED

- Small mixing bowl (cereal bowl)
- Skillet
- Spatula

1. Mix meat and your preference of seasonings and form into a patty. It will shrink a little, so make it a little larger than you want.

2. Fry on medium in your skillet until done. Turn the patty once to brown other side. When you press lightly on the patty with your spatula and the juice is clear it is done.

SERVES: 1

SERVING HINTS: Serve on bread or a bun, you could also just eat it plain. Good served with beans and/or chips.

HAMBURGER STEAK WITH MUSHROOM GRAVY

- ¼ lb. hamburger
- 1/8 cup breadcrumbs
- ½ tsp. onion powder or 2 tbsp. diced onion
- ½ tsp. salt
- ¼ tsp. pepper
- ¼ tsp. Worcestershire sauce
- 1 pkg. dried mushroom gravy or 1 can (10 ¾ oz.) mushroom soup

YOU WILL NEED

- Lg. mixing bowl
- Iron skillet
- Lid
- Spatula
- Lg. spoon

1. Mix all ingredients in bowl. Shape into a large oval patty.

2. Fry on medium until lightly browned, turn over patty with spatula and brown on other

3. side. Turn heat to low.

4. Make gravy according to pkg. instructions or open can of soup and pour over patty. Cover and simmer on low for 10 to 15 minutes.

SERVES: 1

SERVING HINTS: Can be served with those mashed potatoes you can heat in microwave or sit patty on a pile of cooked noodles and pour gravy or both.

HAMBURGER STEW

(Great for a cold and blistery day)

- ½ lb. hamburger
- ½ cup diced onion or ½ tsp. onion powder
- ½ tsp. salt
- ¼ tsp. pepper
- ½ tsp. garlic powder
- 1 can (14.5 oz.) diced tomatoes, undrained
- 1 can (10 ¾ oz.) mushroom soup
- 2 beef cubes
- 1 med. Potato diced (remember you can buy just 1 potato at the store)
- 1 can biscuits, or make your own from your pancake mix

YOUR WILL NEED

- Oven to 350 degrees
- Skillet
- Can opener
- Lg. spoon
- Med. bowl (if you make your own biscuits)

1. Fry hamburger, add spices. Fry until meat is done.

2. Add tomatoes, beef cubes, diced potato and mushroom soup, stir well and simmer until beef cubes have dissolved.

3. Arrange biscuits over top of stew to cover. Put in oven and bake until the biscuits are done (see pkg. directions). They should be a nice golden brown.

SERVES: 2 OR 3

SERVING HINTS: Serve with a side of vegetables and a salad. Better yet add the veggies to the stew before you cover it with the biscuits. (Corn, peas, mixed vegetables or green beans).

HAMBURGER SURPRISE PACKET

Meal in a packet

- ½ lb. hamburger
- ½ tbsp. Worcestershire sauce (optional)
- ½ tsp. garlic powder
- ½ tsp. onion powder or ¼ cup diced onion
- ½ tsp. salt
- ¼ tsp. pepper
- 1 can (15oz) mixed vegetables, drained
- 1 sm. Potato diced small
- 1 tsp. Cajun seasoning or season-all

YOU WILL NEED

- Oven to 450 degrees
- 2 lg. pieces of foil (approx. 12 by 14 inches each)
- Cookie sheet or iron skillet
- Can opener
- Lg. spoon

1. Mix hamburger, Worcestershire sauce, salt, garlic powder, pepper and onion, shape into 2 patties. Place patties onto foil and form foil to resemble a bowl.

2. Top each patty with half of diced potatoes, vegetables and sprinkle everything with the Cajun seasoning or season-all or both. Fold the top of the bowl inward to form a leak proof packet.

3. Place the packets in your skillet or on your cookie sheet and bake for 45 minutes or until hamburger is no longer pink in the center.

SERVES: 2

SERVING HINTS: Eat one and save or freeze the other one for later.

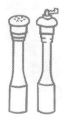

HAMBURGER VEGGIE SOUP

Easy 1 pot meal

- ½ lb. hamburger
- ¼ cup diced onion
- 1 can (15oz.) diced vegetables
- 1 beef cube
- 2 cans (15oz.) diced tomatoes (flavored or plain)
- 1 cup water
- ½ tsp. salt
- ¼ tsp. pepper
- ½ tsp. season-all
- ½ tsp. garlic powder

YOU WILL NEED

- Can opener
- Lg. spoon
- Measuring cup
- Iron skillet

1. Brown hamburger and onions on medium until done.

2. Add rest of ingredients, reduce heat and simmer for 15 to 20 minutes.

SERVES: 2 OR MORE

SERVING HINTS: Serve with crusty bread (Italian) or crackers. If you are really hungry you could also serve this with a salad.

MEATBALLS

Not just for spaghetti

- 1 lb. hamburger
- ½ cup breadcrumbs (Italian) or cracker crumbs
- 1/3 cup parmesan cheese
- 1 tsp. salt
- ½ tsp. pepper
- ¼ tsp. nutmeg (optional)
- 1 lg. egg
- 1 tbsp. Italian seasoning
- 1 tbsp. parsley (optional)
- ½ cup water
- 1/3 cup oil for frying

YOU WILL NEED

- Lg. bowl
- Lg. spoon
- Iron skillet and lid
- Spatula

1. Mix hamburger, crumbs, egg, cheese and seasonings. Mix well.

2. Form into 2 inch balls. Fry in oil on medium. As each "side" gets brown, turn it with your spatula until the whole ball is brown. Turn heat to low.

3. Add water, cover and simmer for another 10 to 20 minutes until the meat is no longer pink in the center.

SERVES: 2 TO 6

SERVING HINTS: Cut in half, sprinkle with extra parmesan cheese and serve as a sandwich. Freeze what you don't eat and use them for spaghetti.

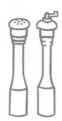

MEATLOAF

Comfort food

- 1 lb. hamburger
- 1 egg
- ½ cup catsup
- ½ tsp. garlic powder
- ½ tsp. salt
- ½ tsp. pepper
- ¾ cup breadcrumbs, rice or cracker crumbs
- ½ tsp. Cajun seasoning or season-all

YOU WILL NEED

- Oven at 350 degrees
- Lg. bowl
- Lg. spoon
- Measuring cup
- Iron skillet
- Foil

1. Mix all ingredients well. Form into an oval shape (football shape for the guys), flatten the ends.

2. Line your pan with foil (for easy clean-up)

3. Bake for 1 hour.

SERVES: 1 TO 4

SERVING HINTS: Serve with a baked potato and baked beans. That way everything can go into the oven at one time. You can add any spices you like. You could also add some diced green peppers (remember the salad bar). Leftovers make great sandwiches.

MEXICAN SKILLET DINNER

1 pot meal

- ½ lb. hamburger
- 1 can (11 oz.) corn, drained
- 1 can (15oz.) diced spicy tomatoes
- ½ cup uncooked instant rice
- 1 can (15 oz.) pinto or kidney beans, drained
- 1 tsp. chili powder
- ¼ tsp. cumin (optional)
- ½ tsp. salt
- ¼ tsp. pepper
- ½ cup shredded Mexican mix cheese

YOU WILL NEED

- Skillet and lid (use foil if you don't have a lid)
- Strainer
- Can opener
- Lg. spoon

1. Fry hamburger on medium until done, add rest of ingredients, except cheese. Cover and simmer about 5 to 10 minutes or until rice is done.

2. Sprinkle with cheese, cover and simmer until cheese is melted, about 5 minutes.

SERVES: 1 TO 4

SERVING HINTS: Serve with a salad. You can also sprinkle broken taco chips over the top (flavored or plain).

PIZZA BURGER

Something different

- ¼ lb. hamburger
- 1 tbsp. pizza sauce
- 1 tbsp. mozzarella cheese (or 1 slice)
- ¼ tsp. salt

YOU WILL NEED

- Iron skillet
- Spatula
- Bowl

1. Divide meat in half and make two thin patties. Put sauce and cheese on one patty and top with the other patty. Pinch the edges of the two patties together.

2. Fry on medium until browned, turn over and brown other side of patty.

SERVES: 1

SERVING HINTS: Serve on a bun or bread. You can pour on more pizza sauce and cheese. A salad or slaw would make a nice side dish.

POOR MAN'S STROGANOFF

- ½ lb. hamburger
- 1 container (4oz.) sour cream
- 1 tbsp. Worchester sauce
- ½ tsp. salt
- ¼ tsp. pepper
- ¼ tsp. garlic powder
- ½ tsp. onion powder or ¼ sm. Diced onion

YOU WILL NEED

- Iron skillet
- Lg. spoon
- Paring knife
- Measuring spoons
- Measuring cup

1. Fry meat on medium, add onion, spices, Worchester sauce and onion. Stir occasionally. When the meat is done turn heat to low.

2. Add sour cream; simmer only until sour cream is warm.

SERVES: 1 OR 2

SERVING HINTS: Serve over noodles, toast or mashed potatoes.

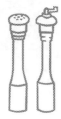

SALSA BEEF SKILLET

1 pot meal

- ½ lb. hamburger
- 8 oz. chunky salsa
- 1 can (15 oz.) kidney beans, undrained
- 1 can (11 oz.) whole kernel corn
- 1 can (4 oz.) tomato sauce
- 1 tsp. chili powder

YOU WILL NEED

- Iron skillet
- Lg. spoon
- Can opener

1. Crumble and fry hamburger until done, stir in salsa, beans, corn, tomato sauce and chili powder. Heat to a boil, reduce heat and simmer for 10 to 15 minutes.

SERVES: 1 OR 2

SERVING HINTS: Serve with crackers or pita bread. If you like cheese, sprinkle with some shredded cheddar.

SHEPHERD PIE

1 pot meal

- ½ lb. hamburger
- ¼ cup onion diced
- 1 can (15 oz.) diced tomatoes
- 1 can (15 oz) mixed vegetables
- ½ tsp. salt
- ¼ tsp. pepper
- ½ tsp. garlic powder
- 2 tbsp. flour
- 1 can (10 ¾ oz.) mushroom soup
- 1 container of mashed potatoes (found in the meat department) thawed

YOU WILL NEED

- Oven to 375 degrees
- Iron skillet
- Lg. spoon
- Can opener
- Measuring spoons

1. Crumble and fry hamburger on medium, add spices.

2. Sprinkle with flour (thickening) and stir until thoroughly mixed.

3. Add tomatoes and vegetables, mix well. Turn heat off.

4. Spread thawed potatoes over top of meat mixture and bake for 15 to 18 minutes.

SERVES: 1 TO 3

SERVING HINTS: If you have some crusty bread it would be fantastic with this dish. You could also add a salad.

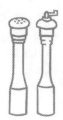

SPAGHETTI SAUCE

Semi-homemade

- 1 jar (24oz.) spaghetti sauce
- 1 can (15oz.) diced Italian tomatoes
- 1 tsp. garlic powder
- ½ tsp. salt
- ½ tsp. oregano (optional)
- 1 tsp. cinnamon (secret ingredient)

YOU WILL NEED

- Lg. saucepan
- Lg. spoon
- Can opener

1. Put all ingredients in pan and simmer on low until they come to a boil.

SERVES: 5 TO 7

SERVING HINTS: Serve over spaghetti and sprinkle with parmesan cheese. You can use any leftover spaghetti and sauce as baked spaghetti (see miscellaneous section). You could also use the sauce to pour over hamburgers. Leftover spaghetti can be made into spaghetti with Alfredo sauce (see miscellaneous section). You can fry and season ½ to 1 pound of hamburger and add to sauce for meat sauce.

SWISS STEAK BURGERS

- ½ lb. hamburger
- ½ tsp. salt
- ¼ tsp. pepper
- ½ tsp. onion powder or ½ cup onion, diced
- 1 can (15oz.) diced tomatoes

YOU WILL NEED

- Iron skillet
- Lg. spoon
- Can opener
- Spatula
- Knife
- Bowl

1. Mix meat and spices, form into two oval patties. Fry on medium until done.

2. Add tomatoes and simmer for 10 to 15 minutes on low.

SERVES: 2

SERVING HINTS: Serve with a vegetable and/or a potato dish. The tomato sauce makes a good gravy or mashed potatoes or leftover rice or noodles.

TACO CASSEROLE

1 pot meal

- ½ lb. hamburger
- ¼ cup onion diced
- ¾ cup uncooked instant rice
- ½ cup picante sauce
- 1 can (15oz.) diced tomatoes, undrained
- 1 can (11oz.) Mexican corn
- 1 can (6oz.) tomato paste

YOU WILL NEED

- Iron skillet with lid
- Lg. spoon
- Mixing bowl
- Knife
- Can opener

1. Brown meat and onion until meat is done.

2. Add rest of ingredients, bring to a boil, stir occasionally.

3. Remove from heat, cover and let rest for 5 minutes.

SERVES: 2 TO 4

SERVING HINTS: Just before you cover the casserole you could sprinkle it with some shredded cheese. When you are ready to eat, sprinkle some crushed up tacos.

TACO SALAD

Crowd pleaser (thanks Sis)

- 1 lb. hamburger
- 1 pkg. taco seasoning
- Water for taco seasoning
- 1 can (15oz.) kidney beans, drained
- 1 can (15oz.) diced tomatoes, drained
- 3 cups lettuce, cut up small (don't forget the salad bar)
- 6 oz. shredded cheddar cheese
- ½ pkg. Fritos
- 1 sm. Bottle of French dressing

YOU WILL NEED

- Iron skillet
- Lg. spoon
- Mixing bowl

1. Crumble and fry hamburger, add taco seasoning and water, simmer on low for 4 to 6 minutes, turn heat off.

2. Mix lettuce, beans, tomatoes and cheese, add meat mixture.

3. Sprinkle Fritos over top.

SERVES: 3 TO 5

SERVING HINTS: This is a meal in a pot.

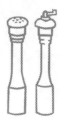

TOASTED HAMBURGER

Done in the broiler

- ½ lb. hamburger
- ½ bottle (17oz) BBQ sauce
- ½ tsp. onion powder or ¼ cup diced onion
- ½ tsp. garlic powder
- 1 tsp. Worcestershire sauce
- 4 buns or 4 slices bread

YOU WILL NEED

- Oven on broil
- Foil
- Cookie sheet pan
- Spatula
- Bowl
- Lg. spoon

1. Mix all ingredients (except bread) and spread on half a bun or slice of bread.

2. Arrange buns or bread, with filling on foil lined cookie sheet and place in broiler. Broil for 15 to 20 min. or until done. Watch them as they are under an open flame.

SERVES: 4

SERVING HINTS: Serve with chips and a salad.

MISCELLANEOUS

HINTS

1. Purchase thick sliced bologna at the deli section of the grocery.

2. Acquire fresh vegetables, in small portions at the salad bar at the grocery, (cauliflower, carrots, broccoli, cut up onions, etc.).

3. Shells and cheese-(macaroni and cheese) use the shells for soup or goulash and use the cheese as a sauce for another recipe.

4. Take any package of flavored side dishes (rice, shells, noodles) and add a package of tuna to make a tasty and quick meal.

If you fry bacon, save the grease and store it covered in the refrigerator. The grease makes for good flavoring in other fried foods. Add one tablespoon of grease to baked beans or green beans, it makes them taste like you have been cooking all day.

BAKED POTATO

- 1 lg. baking potato (yes you can buy 1 potato at the grocery)
- Any topping you like (sour cream, veggies, bacon bits, butter—the list is endless)

1. Wrap potato in small square of foil, place on cookie sheet and bake for 1 hour or until done. Stick knife in potato, if it goes in easily it is done.

SERVES: 1

SERVING HINTS: This can be eaten as a side dish or pile it up to make a 1 dish meal.

You can also fix the potato in a microwave. Puncture the potato with a knife, place on a paper plate or microwave safe dish and heat until done, approx. 5 to 8 min.

BAKED SPAGETTI

Leftovers to love

- 2 cups leftover spaghetti and sauce
- ¼ cup onion, diced
- ½ tsp. garlic powder
- ¼ tsp. salt
- ¼ tsp. pepper
- 1 can (15 oz.) tomatoes (garlic or Italian)
- ½ cup shredded cheddar cheese
- 1/3 cup parmesan cheese

YOU WILL NEED

- Oven at 325 degrees
- Iron skillet with lid
- Lg. spoon
- Can opener
- Measuring cup and spoons

1. Put all ingredients, except parmesan cheese, in skillet and mix well. Sprinkle with parmesan.

2. Cover and bake for 30 minutes or until hot, uncover and bake for another 15 minutes.

SERVES: 3 TO 4

SERVING HINTS: This would be good alone or with salad.

BBQ CANNED LUNCHEON MEAT

Easy

- 1 tin (7 oz.) luncheon meat
- Leftover BBQ sauce
- 1 Tbsp. oil or spray oil

YOU WILL NEED

- Skillet
- Knife
- Spatula

1. Remove meat from tin and slice as thick or thin as you like. Place oil in skillet and put in slices of meat. Fry on medium until browned on both sides.

2. Pour BBQ sauce over meat and simmer until sauce is hot.

SERVES: 1 OR 2

SERVING HINTS: Serve as a sandwich or open faced on one piece of bread. This recipe would go good with chips or French fries.

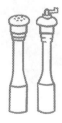

BEER BRATS AND SAUERKRAUT

Good while watching the game

- 1 pkg. brats
- 1 pkg. or lg. can of sauerkraut, drained and rinsed
- 1 can (15oz.) tomatoes, your choice of flavor
- 1 reg. can beer, your favorite
- 2 tbsp. sugar

YOU WILL NEED

- Iron skillet or lg. saucepan with lid
- Lg. spoon
- Can opener

1. Pour beer in pan or skillet. Put in brats, cover pan and cook over medium about ½ hour. Add rest of ingredients and stir, careful to not break your brats. Cover and simmer until sauerkraut is really hot.

SERVES: 2 TO 4

SERVING HINTS: These are good served over mashed potatoes with rye bread. The brats and kraut are good by themselves.

BOILED EGGS

- 2 Eggs
- Water

YOU WILL NEED

- Saucepan
- Lg. spoon

1. Put eggs into saucepan, cover with enough water so it is 1 inch above egg.

2. Cook over medium heat until water boils, turn heat to low.

3. Simmer 2 to 3 minutes for soft-boiled or 10 to 15 minutes for hard-boiled.

4. Remove with spoon and run under cold water.

5. Crack shell on counter top and rotate the egg as you crack it. Peel, eat and enjoy. Start peeling the egg at the big end as there is a small air space which makes it easier to start the peeling.

SERVES: 1

SERVING HINTS: You can eat the eggs with salt and pepper or you can cut them up and put them on a salad. You can also make egg salad (see Index).

CALZONES

- 1 pkg. tuna, or ½ cup cooked ham or ½ cup cooked chicken
- ½ cup shredded sharp cheese
- ½ can (15oz.) diced tomatoes, drained (save juice and other half of tomatoes)
- ½ cup onion, diced
- 3 cups pancake/biscuit mix
- ½ cup water
- 2 tbsp. oil
- 2 tbsp. milk

YOU WILL NEED

- Oven to 450 degrees
- Mixing bowl
- Cookie sheet
- Can opener
- Lg. spoon
- Foil

Salsa Cheese Sauce
- Heat remaining tomatoes, juice and ½ cup shredded cheese in micro or saucepan.

1. Mix meat, cheese, tomatoes and onion in one bowl.

2. Stir pancake/biscuit mix, water and oil to form a ball, knead a few times until ball holds together. Sprinkle a little pancake/biscuit mix on foil. Put ball in center and pat or roll out to about a 12 inch circle.

3. Pour mixture onto half of the circle, fold over and pinch edges together. Place on foil covered cookie sheet and bake for 20 to 30 minutes or until golden brown.

SERVES: 1 OR 2

SERVING HINTS: Cut into wedges and top with sauce. Serve with a salad to round out the meal.

COCKTAIL SAUCE

- ½ cup catsup
- 1 tbsp. horseradish (more if you like it really hot)
- Splash of lemon juice (optional)

YOU WILL NEED

- Sm. Mixing bowl
- Spoon

1. Mix all ingredients.

SERVES: 1 TO 6

SERVING HINTS: This sauce is not just for shrimp. You can use it on hamburgers, fish or use it for a dipping sauce for cut up vegetables.

CORN ON THE COB

Microwave

- 1 ear of corn in the husk
  (the mixed, yellow and
  white, corn is sweeter)
- Butter to taste

1. Place corn, still in husk, on plate and sprinkle with a little
   water.

2. Cover plate with plastic wrap and microwave for 3 min.

SERVES: 1

SERVING HINTS: Each ear of corn takes 3 minutes. So if you do the math, 4 ears would have to cook for 12 minutes. An easy way to butter your corn is to slather a slice of bread and roll the ear of corn on the bread. The husk and silk come off the really easy after being micro waved.

CREAMED PEAS

- 1 can (15oz.) peas
- 2 tbsp. flour
- 1 tbsp. butter
- ½ tsp. salt
- ¼ tsp. pepper

YOU WILL NEED

- Saucepan
- Can opener
- Lg. spoon

1. Pour peas into saucepan, sprinkle with flour, and stir well. Add spices and butter. Heat until the sauce becomes thick. Stir constantly or the flour will settle to the bottom of the pan and stick.

SERVES: 1 TO 4

SERVING HINTS: I pour creamed peas over my salmon patties. They also go well with ham, pork or chicken. If they don't thicken up a lot you can always add a little more flour---but stir well or you will have clumps of flour in your peas.

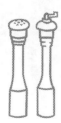

CUCUMBER SALAD

Refreshing

- 1 sm. Cucumber, peeled
- 1 sm. Onion, peeled and sliced into rings
- ¼ cup mayonnaise
- 2 tbsp. vinegar
- 2 tbsp. sugar
- ½ tsp. salt
- ½ tsp. pepper

YOU WILL NEED

- 2 Mixing bowls
- Lg. spoon
- Knife
- Plastic wrap

1. Slice peeled cucumber and onion into thin (¼ inch) slices. Put into the bowl.

2. Mix mayonnaise, vinegar, sugar and spices, mix well. Pour over cucumbers and onions.

3. Cover and refrigerate until chilled, about 1 hour.

SERVES: 1 TO 3

SERVING HINTS: This is a very refreshing salad in the summer but can be eaten any time. It is even better the second day.

EGG SALAD

Easy

- 3 eggs
- 2 tbsp. mayonnaise
- ½ tsp. salt
- ¼ tsp. pepper
- 1 tbsp. sweet pickle relish
- ¼ cup onion, diced (optional)

YOU WILL NEED

- Saucepan
- Lg. spoon
- Knife

1. Put eggs in saucepan and cover with cold water. Bring to a boil and continue to boil for 20 minutes.

2. Remove from heat and rinse with cold water until cool enough to handle. Crack and roll eggs on counter top and peel.

3. Dice eggs into about ½ inch pieces. Add rest of ingredients, stir to mix. Refrigerate.

SERVES: 1 TO 3

SERVING HINTS: Pile on bread and have it as a sandwich, serve it on crackers as a snack or eat it all by itself.

FETTUCCINI ALFREDO

Easy

- 1 pkg. (3 oz.) cream cheese
- 1/3 cup parmesan cheese
- ½ cup butter
- ¼ cup milk
- 4 oz. cooked drained fettuccini or spaghetti (you can also use leftover spaghetti)

1. Put cream cheese, parmesan cheese, butter and milk in saucepan, heat on low stirring constantly, or it will stick. When the cream cheese has melted toss in the cooked spaghetti.

SERVES: 1

SERVING HINTS: Being a cheese lover, I always add more parmesan cheese at the when it is piled up on my plate. If it is to thin add more parmesan, if to thick add more butter or milk.

FRANKS AND SAUERKRAUT

Fast and easy

- 1 can (15oz.) sauerkraut, rinsed
- 2 hot dogs
- 2 tbsp. sugar

YOU WILL NEED

- Saucepan
- Lg. spoon
- Can opener

1. Put hot dogs in just enough water to cover them, cook for 10 to 15 minutes or until done.

2. Add rinsed sauerkraut and sugar, simmer until sauerkraut is hot. (The longer it cooks the better it is.)

SERVES: 1

SERVING HINTS: You can eat this alone or with mashed potatoes. Rye bread goes well with sauerkraut.

FRENCH FRIES

Seasoned

- 1 lg. baking potato, washed, cut into 3/8 inch strips
- 1/8 cup oil
- ½ tsp. salt
- ½ tsp. pepper
- ½ tsp. garlic powder
- ½ tsp. season-all

YOU WILL NEED

- Oven to 425 degrees
- Foil lined cookie sheet
- Lg. plastic zippered bag
- Spatula
- Knife

1. Put oil, seasonings and potato strips in the plastic bag, seal and shake well. Put seasoned potatoes onto lined cookie sheet.

2. Bake for 25 minutes. Turn the potatoes over with the spatula and bake another 10 minutes or until done. (They are done when the end of a sharp knife goes into the fries easily).

SERVES: 1

SERVING HINTS: Good with any sandwich or meat that you like. Make a meal out of the fries buy adding chili and cheese. You can also add parmesan cheese to the seasonings.

FRIED CORN

- 3 tbsp. butter
- 1 can (15oz) whole corn, drained
- 3 tbsp. sugar
- ¼ cup milk
- ½ tsp. salt
- ¼ tsp. pepper

YOU WILL NEED

- Iron skillet
- Lg. spoon
- Can opener

1. Melt butter in skillet on medium

2. Stir in drained corn, cook for about a minute. Add sugar and milk and cook for another minute.

3. Increase heat and add milk, stir constantly to keep the corn from sticking. Add seasonings. Cook until most of the milk has been absorbed by the corn. About 4 to 5 minutes.

SERVES: 1 TO 4

SERVING HINTS: This is a good side dish to any meat you serve. I tried it with leftover bacon grease (about 1 tbsp.), instead of butter and it was really good.

FRUITY CREAM CHEESE SPREAD

- 1 3 oz. pkg. cream cheese, softened (let set out for at least 1 hour)
- 2 tbsp jam or preserves (use your favorite flavor)

YOU WILL NEED

- Sm. Mixing bowl
- Spoon

1. Mix two ingredients well. (store leftovers in refrigerator)

SERVES: 1 TO 4

SERVING HINTS: Serve on crackers for a sweet treat or spread some on a piece of bread for a quick sandwich.

ICED TEA

Strong and sweet

- 11 single tea bags
- 1 cup sugar
- 8 cups water

YOU WILL NEED

- Saucepan
- Long spoon
- 64 oz. pitcher
- Measuring cup

1. Put two cups of the water in the saucepan, add the tea bags (remove all tags).

2. While the tea is coming to a boil add another two cups of water to the pitcher and add the sugar.

3. When the tea is done steeping and using your spoon as a stopper for the tea bags, pour the tea into the sugar water. Stir. Add two cups more of water to the tea bags in the sauce pan. Repeat this until your pitcher is full. Let cool and put in the refrigerator.

SERVES: 1 TO 6

SERVING HINTS: If you don't like your tea this strong, just eliminate a tea bag or two. You can also add a splash of lemon.

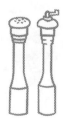

MASHED POTATO CANDY

No cooking involved

- ¼ cup leftover mashed potatoes
- ½ cup peanut butter
- 1 box (1 pound) confectionary sugar

YOU WILL NEED

- Mixing bowl
- Lg. spoon
- Butter knife
- Foil
- Rolling pin or foil lined food can

1. Put mashed potatoes into bowl, slowly add confectionary sugar and stir as you add. Keep adding sugar until the mixture is stiff enough to roll out, like pizza dough.

2. Place foil on counter and sprinkle with a little confectionary sugar. Place potato ball onto foil and roll out until about ½ inch thick.

3. Spread peanut butter over entire surface. Starting at one side, roll the mixture up into a cylinder. Put into refrigerator for 1 hour.

4. Cut cylinder into 1 inch pieces and serve.

SERVES: 1 TO 4

SERVING HINTS: Use as a dessert-why not? This candy is sweet and makes a perfect ending to a meal. It also makes a great snack while you are sitting doing your homework or paperwork.

OVEN ROASTED POTOTO WEDGES

- 1 lg. baking potato
- ½ tsp. onion powder
- ¼ tsp. garlic powder
- ½ tsp. salt
- ¼ tsp. pepper
- ¼ cup parmesan cheese
- ½ tsp. Cajun seasoning or hot sauce
- 1/3 cup oil

YOU WILL NEED

- Oven to 375 degrees
- Iron skillet
- Lg. plastic zip bag
- Spatula

1. Cut potato into ½ inch wedges, lengthwise. You don't have to peel the potato.

2. Put spices, potatoes and oil into the plastic bag, seal and shake the bag to cover all the potatoes.

3. Pour into skillet and spread out. Bake uncovered for 40 minutes, toss occasionally. Sprinkle with parmesan cheese and bake for another 10 minutes or until tender.

SERVES: 1

SERVING HINTS: If you don't do "hot" just omit the hot sauce. Good with any sandwich or meat you like.

PITA PIZZA

- 2 lg. pitas, without pockets
- ½ cup of pizza sauce
- ¼ cup onion, diced
- ½ tsp. garlic powder
- ½ cup shredded cheese, your choice (remember the salad bar)
- ¼ cup leftover meat or pepperoni

YOU WILL NEED

- Oven to 400 degrees
- Foil lined cookie sheet
- Spatula
- Measuring cup

1. Place pitas on foil lined cookie sheet and spread with pizza sauce.

2. Spread other ingredients evenly over pitas

3. Sprinkle with cheese and bake in oven until cheese is melted, about 10 to 15 minutes.

SERVES: 1 OR 2

SERVING HINTS: Eat one and refrigerate one for tomorrow's dinner. Remember, add any ingredients you like to have on a pizza. These go well with a salad or chips.

PIZZA DOUGH

3 versions

- 3 cups pancake mix
- 2/3 cup water
- 2 tbsp. oil
- ½ tsp. garlic powder
- 1/3 cup parmesan cheese

YOU WILL NEED

- Oven at 425 degrees
- Cookie sheet, oiled
- Pizza knife
- Bowl

1. Mix pancake mix, water and oil until it forms a rough ball. Let stand for 7 minutes.

2. Put dough ball on oiled cookie sheet and spread to the edges, using your hands. Oil hands to keep the dough from sticking.

3. Add all your favorite toppings and bake for 15 to 20 minutes.

SERVES: 1 TO 6

SERVING HINTS: This is your pizza so use your imagination and go wild with the toppings. Don't forget the salad bar.

- **VERSION 2:** Refrigerated biscuits can be flattened to ¼ to ½ inch, cover with toppings and bake for 10 minutes or until crust is golden.

- **VERSION 3:** Break apart English muffins, add toppings and bake at 350 degrees for 10 minutes.

POTATO PATTY

Leftover mashed potatoes

- 1 cup leftover mashed potatoes
- 1 egg
- 1/8 cup finely diced onion
- 2 tbsp. flour or pancake mix
- ¼ tsp. salt
- 3 tbsp. oil, bacon grease or butter

YOU WILL NEED

- Skillet
- Spatula
- Bowl
- Spoon
- Measuring cup and spoons

1. Mix mashed potatoes; egg, salt, onion and flour in bowl Form patties with your hands. If they seem to wet add some more flour.

2. Place patties in melted oil or grease and fry over medium heat until browned. Flip them over and brown other side.

SERVES: 1

SERVING HINTS: This potato patty is good with any meal. I might even try a little parmesan cheese in or on it.

QUICK SNACKS

Finger food

1. Popcorn-sprinkled with parmesan cheese.

2. Nachos-canned tomatoes with chilies for dipping.

3. Raw vegetables-remember that salad bar (carrots, celery, green peppers, cauliflower, and broccoli). The salad bars also have little cups to carry your favorite dressings for dipping.

4. Cheese and crackers.

5. Peanut butter and crackers.

6. Fresh fruit

SALMON PATTIES

- 1 can (15oz.) pink salmon, drained and cleaned
- ½ sleeve of round buttery crackers, crumbled
- 2 eggs, beaten
- ½ tsp. salt
- 1/8 cup oil for cooking

YOU WILL NEED

- Iron skillet
- Spatula
- Bowl
- Spoon
- Can opener
- Fork

1. Put drained cleaned salmon (break salmon in half lengthwise and remove the spines and the black skin) in the bowl. Add the eggs, crackers and salt. Form into 4 patties.

2. Fry on low to medium heat until one side is browned, flip over and brown other side.

SERVES: 1 TO 4

SERVING HINTS: I spoon creamed peas (see Index) over my patties, but you could use a cheese sauce. Even a tarter sauce would be good on them. Add a side of salad and you have a fantastic meal.

SOFT PRETZELS

Salty or sweet

- 1 loaf frozen white bread, thawed
- ¼ cup flour or pancake mix for dusting
- 1 egg, beaten
- ½ cup sea salt
- Toppings: cinnamon & sugar, sea salt, garlic powder, parmesan cheese

YOU WILL NEED

- Oven to 400 degrees
- Lg. saucepan, ¾ full of water, heated to boiling
- Foil lined cookie sheet
- Spatula
- Paper towels
- Sharp knife

1. Divide thawed bread dough into 12 pieces, cut with a knife. On floured surface, roll dough with hands into a long 14 inch rope and form into a pretzel shape.

2. While water is boiling carefully ease the pretzels in the water two at a time. When they rise to the surface remove with your spatula and place on paper towels to drain. Boil remaining pretzels and drain.

3. Arrange boiled pretzels on foil lined cookie sheet, about 2 inches apart and brush them with the beaten egg (you can use your fingers if you don't have a pastry brush).

4. Sprinkle with toppings of your choice (half sweet and half salty) and bake for 15 to 20 minutes or until golden brown. When they are cool store them in a lidded container.

SERVES: 1 TO 6

SERVING HINTS: Have some yellow mustard in a bowl for spreading or dipping. Great while watching the big game or doing homework. Have fun with the toppings, mix and match.

TUNA BAKE

Fast and easy

- 1 pkg. tuna
- 1 can (10 ¾ oz) mushroom soup
- 1 can (15 oz.) mixed vegetables
- ½ tsp. salt
- ½ tsp. pepper
- ¼ cup shredded cheddar cheese or a small handful

YOU WILL NEED

- Oven to 425 degrees
- Iron skillet
- Lg. spoon
- Can opener

1. Mix all ingredients in skillet, put in oven and bake for 20 to 30 minutes.

SERVES: 1 TO 5

SERVING HINTS: You could add diced onion to this to liven up the flavor. Serve with a salad and crackers.

TUNA SALAD

Refreshing and quick

- 1 pkg. tuna
- 2 tbsp. mayonnaise
- 2 tbsp. sweet pickle relish
- 2 tbsp. onion, diced
- ¼ tsp. salt

YOU WILL NEED

- Mixing bowl
- Fork
- Measuring spoons

1. Mix all ingredients, you can eat it right away or chill it for an hour.

SERVES: 1 TO 4

SERVING HINT: You can eat this as a meat dish, sandwich or on crackers.

PORK

BREADED PORK CHOP

- 2 loin pork chops
- ½ sleeve round buttery crackers, crushed
- 1 egg, beaten
- 1/8 cup oil

YOU WILL NEED

- Oven to 350 degrees
- 2 sm. Bowls
- Iron skillet
- Cookie sheet
- Foil
- Fork

1. Heat skillet, put beaten egg in one bowl and the cracker crumbs in the other, dip chops into beaten egg and coat both sides.

2. Dip coated chops into cracker crumbs and coat both sides well.

3. Fry on low until crackers are golden brown on both sides. Just turn once.

4. Take foil and crumple to form a "plate" for the chops and place on cookie sheet, bake for 1 hour, uncovered.

SERVES: 1 TO 2

SERVING HINTS: Baked beans and a baked potato complete this meal. The chops are really tender. You can add some spices to the cracker crumbs.

CAJUN PORK BURGER

- ½ lb. ground pork (use the other half for chili)
- ¼ cup diced onion or ½ tsp. onion powder
- ½ tsp. garlic powder
- 1 t. thyme (optional)
- ½ tsp. cayenne or hot sauce
- ¼ tsp. salt
- ¼ tsp. pepper

YOU WILL NEED

- Mixing bowl
- Fork
- Iron skillet
- Spatula

1. Mix all ingredients and shape into patties. Fry on medium heat until lightly browned, flip it over and brown the other side (6 to 7 min. on each side).

SERVES: 1-2

SERVING HINTS: This patty would be good all by itself or as a sandwich. Serve with French fries or chips.

ORANGE PORK CHOPS

- 1 pork chop
- ½ cup orange marmalade (use the rest for bagels or toast)
- ½ tsp. cinnamon (optional)
- ½ cup pancake mix
- ½ tsp. salt
- ¼ tsp. pepper
- ¼ tsp. garlic powder
- 2 tbsp. water or soy sauce
- 1/8 cup oil, for frying

1. Mix pancake mix and dry spices.

2. Coat pork chop with water or soy sauce, dredge with dry ingredients and fry on medium until browned, flip over and brown other side.

3. Mix marmalade and cinnamon and spread over the chop.

SERVES: 1

SERVING HINTS: This would be good served with sweet potatoes and a salad with a sweet dressing. If your chop is not tender enough, cover with foil and put it in the oven at 350 degrees for about 45 minutes.

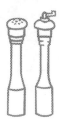

PORK ROAST WITH SAUERKRAUT

Company dinner

- 1 small pork loin roast
- ½ tsp. garlic powder
- ½ tsp. salt
- ½ tsp. pepper
- 1 small onion, diced
- 1 can (15oz.) tomatoes, diced, flavored (your choice)
- 1 can (15oz) sauerkraut, drained and rinsed
- 1 pkg. frozen mashed potatoes (optional)

YOU WILL NEED

- Oven at 350 degrees
- Iron skillet with lid or foil lid
- Fork
- Knife
- Can opener

1. Put roast in skillet and put in oven until it is good and browned, about 1 hour. (I start mine early, about 10 AM in the morning so it can slow cook all day and be super tender).

2. When browned, after an hour or so, add the rest of the ingredients stir them around. Cover and cook until tender, about 4 hours or so. (You now have time to study or clean the apartment, when you are done, so is supper.

SERVES: 1 TO 5

SERVING HINTS: Serve the roast and sauerkraut over the mashed potatoes or alone. Rye bread goes well with sauerkraut.

PORK ROAST

Study dinner

- 1 small pork loin roast
- ½ tsp. garlic powder
- ½ tsp. salt
- 1 tsp. onion powder or ½ cup onion, diced
- ½ tsp. pepper
- 2 or 3 medium potatoes cut into fourths
- 1 sm. Bag baby carrots
- 1 cup water or chicken broth

YOU WILL NEED

- Oven at 350 degrees
- Iron skillet or roasting pan with lid or foil
- Fork
- Knife

1. Put pork in oven for about an hour to brown it, add spices, water and onion cover and continue to bake for about 4 hours, add carrots and potatoes. Bake another 1 to 1 ½ hours until carrots are tender. Check every once in awhile to make sure the pan has enough liquid so your food does not burn. I start my roast about 10 AM; put the carrots and potatoes in about 3 PM.

SERVES: 1 TO 5

SERVING HINTS: This is pretty much a meal in one pot. You could add a salad. While it is cooking you have plenty of time to do work around the apartment or finish that homework.

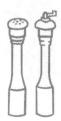

PULLED PORK SANDWICHES

Leftover pork roast

- ½ cooked pork roast, pulled into bite size pieces
- ½ cup pork juice, from the roast
- 1 can (14.5 oz) tomatoes with jalapenos, undrained
- 1 can (4oz) tomato sauce
- 1/3 cup light brown sugar
- 1/3 cup cider vinegar
- 1/3 cup ketchup
- 1/8 tsp. hot sauce (optional)

YOU WILL NEED

- Mixing bowl
- Iron skillet
- Foil
- Can opener
- Measuring cup

1. Mix tomatoes, tomato sauce, sugar, vinegar, ketchup and hot sauce in your skillet.

2. Add pork and pork juice, cover and simmer on low for 30 minutes.

SERVES: 1 TO 3

SERVING HINTS: Spoon over bread for an open faced sandwich. This is good with Cole slaw (don't forget the salad bar).

SAUSAGE AND BAKED BEANS

Fast and easy

- ½ pkg. smoked kielbasa sausage (freeze the other half)
- 1 can (15oz.) baked beans
- 1 tbsp. sugar
- ½ tsp. salt
- 2 tbsp. ketchup

YOU WILL NEED

- Iron skillet
- Knife
- Lg. spoon
- Can opener

1. Put all ingredients in skillet and simmer on low for about 15 to 20 minutes. The sausage should be pre-cooked when you buy it, if not fry the sausage and then add the other ingredients.

SERVES: 1 TO 3

SERVING HINTS: This can be a meal in one pot. If you are extra hungry or have company add fried potatoes or French fries to the menu.

SPICED PORK CHOPS AND SWEET POTATOES

- 2 pork loin chops
- 2 tbsp. oil
- ½ tsp. salt
- ½ tsp. pepper
- ½ cup onion, diced or ½ tsp. onion powder
- 1 can (15oz.) sweet potatoes
- 1 sm. Apple, peeled, cored and cut into cubes, (don't forget the salad bar)
- ¼ cup butter
- 2 tbsp. brown sugar
- 2 tbsp. water
- 1 tsp. cinnamon

YOU WILL NEED

- Oven at 350 degrees
- Iron skillet
- Can opener
- Knife

1. Fry chops in oil on medium until browned on both sides. Turn burner off.

2. Add spices, onions, sweet potatoes and cover with apples.

3. Put pieces of butter around the top of the apples, add brown sugar, water and cinnamon, cover and bake 45 to 55 minutes.

SERVES: 1 OR 2

SERVING HINTS: This is a meal in one pot. Add a side vegetable if you like

MENUS AND SHOPPING LISTS

WEEKLY MENUS & SHOPPING LISTS

MENU	SHOPPING LIST
1. Hamburger patty	• 1 lb. hamburger
2. Chili	• 2 Chicken Breasts, boneless
3. Chicken Strips	• 2 pkg tuna
4. Chicken Sandwich	• Eggs
5. Tuna Salad	• 1 small jar pickle relish
6. Tuna Casserole	• 1 can chili starter
7. Leftovers	• Noodles
	• Bread

MENU	SHOPPING LIST
1. Poor man's stroganoff	• 1 lb. hamburger
2. Toasted hamburger	• 1 lg. ham steak
3. Ham and sweet potatoes	• 1 sm. Chuck roast
4. Roast	• 1 sm. Can sweet potatoes
5. Roast beef sandwiches	• 1 sm. Container sour cream
6. Ham salad	• 1 bottle BBQ sauce
7. Leftovers	

MENU	SHOPPING LIST
1. Pork & sauerkraut	• 1 sm. Pork loin roast
2. Pulled pork Sandwiches	• 1 sm. Can sauerkraut
3. Meatloaf	• 1 lb. hamburger
4. Meatloaf sandwiches	• Spaghetti
5. Spaghetti with meat sauce	• Spaghetti sauce
6. Spaghetti, baked	• Parmesan cheese
7. Leftovers	

MENU	SHOPPING LIST
1. Chuck roast	• lb. chuck roast
2. Beef sandwich	• med. potatoes
3. Chili	• lb. hamburger
4. Beef and noodles	• sm. Pkg. egg noodles
5. Hot dogs with chili sauce	• oz pkg. sour cream
6. Poor man's stroganoff with noodles	• pkg. hot dogs
7. Leftovers	

MENU	SHOPPING LIST
1. Hot dogs with beans	• can (z.) baked beans
2. Loaded baked potato	• Toppings from salad bar (for potato)
3. Ham au gratin	• ham steak
4. Ham sandwich	• can (z.) soup, your
5. Hot dogs and soup	• box au gratin potatoes
6. Hamburger patty	
7. Leftovers	

MENU	SHOPPING LIST
1. Shells and cheese with hamburger	• box shells and cheese
2. Chicken breast	• chicken breasts
3. Chicken nuggets	• lb. hamburger
4. Hamburger patty	• ½ dozen eggs
5. Egg salad	• pork loin chops
6. Breaded pork chop	• buttery round crackers
7. Leftovers	

INDEX

If the recipe has an asterisk (*)
in front of the name, it is a one pot meal.

CHICKEN, 1-18

CHUCK ROAST, 19-27

DESSERTS, 29-40

HAM, 41-51

HAMBURGER, 53-79

BBQ meatloaf, 54

Beef cheesy nachos, 55

*Beef tostados, 56

Cajun burger, 57

*Chili, 58

*Goulash, 59

*Hamburger casserole, 60

*Hamburger cheese pie, 61

Hamburger gravy, 62

Hamburger patty, 63

Hamburger steak with mushroom gravy, 64

*Hamburger stew, 65

*Hamburger surprise packet, 66

*Hamburger veggie soup, 67

Meatballs, 68

Meatloaf, 69

*Mexican skillet, 70

Pizza burger, 71

Poor man's stroganoff, 72

*Salsa beef skillet, 73

*Shepherd pie, 74

Spaghetti sauce, 75

Swiss steak burger, 76

*Taco casserole, 77

*Taco salad, 78

Toasted hamburgers, 79

MISCELLANEOUS, 81-108

Baked potato, 82

Baked spaghetti, 83

BBQ canned luncheon meat, 84

Beer brats with sauerkraut, 85

Boiled eggs, 86

*Calzones, 87

Cocktail sauce, 88

Corn on the cob, 89

Creamed peas, 90

Cucumber salad, 91

Egg salad, 92

*Fettuccini Alfredo, 93

Franks and sauerkraut, 94

French fries, 95

Fried corn, 96

Fruity cream cheese spread, 97

Iced tea, 98

Mashed potato candy, 99

Oven roasted potato wedges, 100

*Pita pizza, 101

Pizza dough, 102

Potato patty, 103

Quick snacks, 104

Salmon patty, 105

Soft pretzels, 106

*Tuna bake, 107

*Tuna salad, 108

PORK, 109-117